Parable Hunter

Parable Hunter

POEMS BY RICARDO PAU-LLOSA

CARNEGIE MELLON UNIVERSITY PRESS
PITTSBURGH 2008

ACKNOWLEDGMENTS

Grateful acknowledgment is made to the magazines and anthologies where these poems first appeared: *Bellingham Review*: "Brújula"; *Boulevard*: "Metrozoo, Miami"; *Colorado Review*: "Cellophane, Marlboro Lights"; *Crab Orchard Review*: "For the Cuban Dead"; *Cream City Review*: "Bogotá, Barrio Norte"; *The Fiddlehead*: "Ibises, Miami"; *Iowa Review*: "Nests, Nearing Key Largo"; *Manoa*: "Immigrant Parable: Hong Kong Orchid Tree, Arguments"; *Massachusetts Review*: "Bulletin Board"; *Mid-American Review*: "Swingline," "Odds"; *New England Review*: "Seven Mile Bridge, Florida Keys"; *North American Review*: "The Good Earth, the Good Stars"; *Painted Bride Quarterly*: "Walking Past a New Five-Story Parking Garage"; *Passages North*: "Offshore Island, Florida Keys"; *Ploughshares*: "Samurai"; *Rattle*: "Abacus"; *Red, White & Blues* [U Iowa Press, 2004]: "Quilt Complex"; *Rhino*: "Ryman Auditorium, Nashville"; *Salmagundi*: "Famine"; *South Dakota Review*: "American Casino"; *Southern Review*: "Seven"; *32 Poems*: "Bitterness"; *TriQuarterly*: "Conjuring Bear," "Winter Landscape with a Bird Trap," "Hunters in the Snow," "The Rice Bird," "Parable Hunter," "Titian's Danae"; *Valparaiso Poetry Review*: "Flight to L.A."; *Writing the Future* [Terra Nova/MIT Press, 2004]: "Progress." "Samurai" was also published in *180 More Extraordinary Poems for Every Day*, ed. Billy Collins, New York: Random House, 2005. "For the Cuban Dead" was also published in *Burnt Sugar/Caña Quemada*, ed. Lori Marie Carlson & Oscar Hijuelos, New York: Free Press, 2006.

Artwork photo by Rolando Valdez/Blue Door Gallery.

Book design: Erika Holmquist

The publication of this book is supported by a grant from the Pennsylvania Council on the Arts.

Library of Congress Control Number: 2007931373
ISBN-13: 978-0-88748-483-4 Pbk.

10 9 8 7 6 5 4 3 2 1

PENNSYLVANIA
COUNCIL
ON THE

ARTS

CONTENTS

4:    ABOUT

For my father
and all other Cubans who have died
in Exile

I: WITHOUT

APPROACHING STORM

after the painting by Constant Troyon

In reds and blues, to contrast with the warning
twist of olive oak and pumice cloud, the travelers
advance on the last ferry to cross the polished river.

The mother, the wife, the child by the hand,
the gentleman or the farmer too tired to hold
nature to account — it is all water, after all,

the lake calm of the river, the arsenal ease of grasses
vigilant and spired, sure as law that rain
is coming and no sun will rob them of that.

The ferryman's staff points to the last blue gash
in what will return as the punctual sky.
On the other shore, another ferryman's arc

is held to signal a window of light in the dense
moil of groves bannered by the speed
of what is just arriving, wind heralded,

and the sky's light is a silver we inhale.
Breath is a peace pipe, for that is what we yearn
from nature. A little shelter. A little time.

Something for our table. And do not let
the lava and the wind and the quake
dictate whims we dread to the mitre

and the crown. O look upon us, Father,
your storms at our back, our storms
humming within us, biding their time.

BRÚJULA

after the drawings and paintings of aloe plants by Julio Rosado del Valle

Since Solomon
we make justice happen
by halves. Day and night
and sex — the hammock
of unity we pray
for our world.
The leaf articulates
what it cannot provide —
mouth and vulva, the pleasures
of birth and speech.
Have faith in halves,
in severed symmetries,
the leaf seems to say.
Don Julio has set a course
for these forms,
between fishing boats
and lips and lids,
so these halves can tell
a punctual tale.
The world is losses,
but measured.
And it hides from the artist,
who has learned another
judgment
than that of the infant king,
his stage gilded
with mothers torn
by want and hope.
There is a spinning
that sets another light

in bloom. The aloe,
compass of all needles,
guides the way.

BITTERNESS

Taste as prophesy,
heraldic perfume

waiting in the mind's nose
to spring forth,

taint the world
as its signature.

Who does not already know
the people he will become?

Pins in the alley,
in the gutter pins.

The ball growls thickly
down the groove —

its marble sentence
syntax free.

Bitterness is a broken abacus
whose beads yearn for the feet of swine.

Mirror is the page
no one can turn.

We all sit at the banquet
eyeing the host's empty chair.

NESTS, NEARING KEY LARGO

On the way down I tell my wife what she'll be seeing:
dozens of nests on old wooden electrical posts,
guarded by wardens, for osprey
and other fishing birds, because there are so few trees,
been blown away by hurricanes.
But when we drive through we only see
one or two poles.
I remembered abundance.
Must have rotted away. Dread to think
the birds have died or gone, wary
of umbrellas and binoculars, the flashing
hoods and the smoking engines.
Tired of our awe and wish, bored
of us who want the nests to burst with the new,
dream the beaks shiny with salt and fish blood,
the trees aflame with spring's tenacity.
We want so much.

ABACUS

Havana 1933, 1954, Miami 2002
for Nicolás, the last of the Cubans

Melancholy is a sin, really it is a sin, instar omnium, for not to will
deeply and sincerely is sin, and this is the mother of all sins.
       — Kierkegaard, *Guilty/Not Guilty*

They were dancing on the roof of the house
next door, flames leaping from the windows,

in the calm metronome of a danzón,
or maybe the mob were clicking their heels

savagely, not, therefore, a dance properly,
but a sudden shaping of flesh to the clay

of vengeful joy. A boy of eight is straying
the opulent streets to amaze at the inkness

of blood on pavement, how it oils the asphalt
into mat provinces the body has seized,

imperial of just dead space, as it quietly fell,
broke and rag turned. The boy had never heard

such silence on this street. Now a grandfather,
Nicolás Quintana is writing his memoirs.

He'd build some of Cuba's vanguard homes and buildings,
later, decades between this ancient day Machado fell

when Nicolás, then a boy, saw the swarm waltz
on the neighbor's roof, and he pondered their arms

curving and legs jerking straight, bodies spun
as if they'd caught or were still trying to net

the incomparable fish of history. He knew
he'd always fall for the narrow joys. After his tale,

in my living room sixty-eight years after the dance,
I dreamt I had been a man the year of my birth,

forty-eight years ago, and chaos fired up
the schooner wind, whipping wave, slamming

the keel against surf. My new woman on deck,
sunglassed, trim and linened. Filling with liquor,

she might be the muse of history.
She of the Italian scarf flitting in the acetylene wind

of the Gulfstream. We'd be heading back to port
in Havana, to more rum and the climax of air

conditioning, but now she reclined like a tongue
between the lip of clouds and the jaw of cushions,

and tasted the blood metallic sea spray on her face.
Havana sparkled behind her in late fifties summer.

Gleamed like a trumpet just polished. Her turboprop
for New York leaves in the morning. A decade from now

it will be too late to live and too soon to remember.

For in order to escape persecution, each would lightly exchange his
native land for another, as if his own country had been taken by an
enemy.

> — Procopius of Caesarea (c.500-560 c.e.),
> *Secret History (Anecdota)*, tr. Richard Atwater

for Alberto Milián

As a mountain lets its height dictate
its duality, one slope netting rain
while the other crumples into desert,
so the psyche and the creatures it ponders
whether in forests or in dream,
or gathered like bouquets at the zoo.

Twin axe, the weapon of self
cuts with every swing what lies
before and after it. How different
from the cloudy leopard's oversize
teeth that mock the killer's smallness,
or the python's meaty sleeve
folding into groggy hunger.

No beast will let us settle for knowing
facts swarming on a label like flies on carrion.
We walk in the paved swelter of the park,
curvaceous through paths punctuated
by the proper tree, the exact boulder
and lemonade stand, and the detailed bronze
of a nearing species. Hoses dangle from branches,
spray away the summer of our winters.
Everywhere tourists saunter in the naked sun
ignoring the willowy ostrich or kelp giraffe.

They float past the elephant's granite sleep
and the grassland cows with spiral horns
who point their asses at the few
who insist on taking their pictures.

A native among strangers, I become the stranger,
deeper so by the wafts of manure tapir and jungle deer
have laid out on their grounds like picnic blankets.
Signs invite us to penetrate the artificial cave
whose narrow brief darkness ends
on a picture window from which chimp
or tiger can be glimpsed close up in the drag
of rest or tossed like artichokes in sibling play.
They are here for us as we are here for them.
Voyeur and the watched mate in inarticulate function.
Some are driven by inner climate

And others only by what they've known. In my pocket
a friend's concerned letter — I should watch my weight,
exercise. I am, he says, entering late middle age,
and those pounds and that writer's slovenly life
will do to me what it did to him — a scroll of illnesses
and therapies lurk but a leap year away.
He cannot imagine what it's meant to have straggled
countryless since the age of six. No man
should outlive his nation, as I have.
The roaming tourists chat and laugh, and no doubt
think the beasts on their nature seeming mounds,
cage free but moated and fenced, are the luckiest
of their kind. Weighed, vaccinated, and fed, they loom
their expensive sleeps careless of how they're prized.
They will not mate in our paradise, mysteriously,
but puzzle all day at the jagged steel and concrete roofs
on the horizon. Surely they cannot yearn for the dark
menace of plain and forest, pine for the panicked clouds

of herds or the goring hunger of the young hunter.
Surely most would have perished by now in their world,
who keel in an afternoon doze, breading
their bright skins with the right dirt of home.

ODDS

Double its species norm, or thrice,
a great egret combs my slow garden,
neck and head the very fraud of reed
in the willow wind, picking off
the dozed lizard and the rock-still toad.

The size of a woman, or of the shadow
common specimen cast on freeway slopes
or the medians of turgid avenues.
It reigns, the golden beaked and eye,
ignoring the longanimous postman
and me quiet in my dead car
holding the wheel two-handed
as if desire might steer the beast
of awe to make a home on my lawn
and ground the miracle.

Among liriope and bougainvillea
and bird of paradise, prey
in frozen hues among the brotherly shades
hope in their way, too,
the white scythe has reached his plenty,
or that his eye might fail, or
the muscled branch of his leg might crack.

Scared into a jeweled tightness,
they get their wish at mine's expense,
and the bird saunters toward the neighbor's
cream caladiums and a blush
of blue plumbago. His neck crooked
into the outline of an ear. But hunger
has no music, only craft.

BULLETIN BOARD

Absence upon absence
have left a hailwork of staples
biting once corners
of different colored sheets
across the slab sand board.
Like moths on a radiator grill,
the paper bits beneath the tiny rods
are velocity's random kill.
These are the cuneiform of pulling
hands, urgent messages stripped,
the remnants left to highlight the holding
in confetti constellations.
Always old functions
bejewel and scatter to speak again.
The eye climbs these fragments
like newlyweds among ruins
whose name is difficult to pronounce,
sure joy is free from the stitching
called history. Clustering
on this vertical page,
the bits fuse and syntax
careless memory. No one
misses the sheets whose tearing
left beauty and thought
stranded together.

PROGRESS

They are the flood's fingerprints — the lizard
scurrying across a wall, the fly's buzz gelled
in hover, the spider's hairline drift,
the vulture and the albatross and all
the kited wings, all the living things
that bring the sea's unleaden habits
to air and land. Their floated
masteries would a normal practice be
had the rains endured and the whirling
arks never keeled. It is no accident
that when men fled the dense quotidian
to rub the empty stars, they wombed
their weight in freedoms
of untroubled space. Suit bubbled,
tubed to air and duty, they bowed
to the mosquito lighting on a pond,
the mantis and the jay. They homaged
the bat's pendulum and the ant's intact dive
from canopies where serpent and monkey
mirror each other's coil and hold.
The flood, maligned in murderous tales,
was not at all about a hated world.
It was and is a call to disregard the plumb,
as do the dancer's silken veil, the flag
folding like kelp in the just breeze,
the balloons of heat and helium.
Behold the hummingbird who will not forget
water's freedom in a falling world.
It did not have to lift toward emptiness
a moon away from its kind,
and ponder continent and season
in spun blurs eclipsed by a gloved thumb
to understand the stillness of journey.

Once they were men fully because they belonged,
and everywhere they looked and chatted and sipped
a bit of coffee, whisked away a fly with a wrist
or jolted a newspaper readably straight,
or flirted, or worried about the world and where
the damn country was going as a trolley rolled
and curtains dipped and bulged breast-like
and hid again in the proper window. They were
home and citizens of it and dared and loved
and were decent and stole and killed and loved again.
They were home. How like the root in the earth,
the crease in the linen, the wind rending the cloud,
the growl in the hunger, the pavement sprayed
with waves crashing against the sea wall.
How like all right things in the mind of place,
they jostled and failed, learned and betrayed.
Like coins in pockets made for them
they cried stridently or simply tinkled in murmurs,
and it didn't matter if talk or life had substance.
Right of place was substance.

There is no *enough* in exile. Not enough anger,
and the blanket of safety always leaves the feet bare.
And it is here, no matter how clean and golden,
that one learns how different the wrist and the fly
and the shot of wave, how *once* never stops
calling although the law of distance deafens.
Memory is the heart's gravity.
The accent of their children
becomes unbearably alien, a dampness
from the sidewalk creeping past the thin sole
and into the ignored sock. Now nothing
escapes notice and the balance is always against.

And it hits them, these never again composed,
that the time to see and hear was then,
when rightness held even the stormy evils
of the quotidian in the same palm
with the trash of years of seconds
and the kissed joys.
Then, as we have come to know, was
the proper place to gaze at the dust
of butterfly panoplies, ponder
the calligraphic crud on china,
relinquish decorous ears to taut goatskins,
wash in the lace of Sunday clouds,
and otherwise pay attention
with one's whole life to shadows
knitting five centuries of incomparable capital,
field's antique jewel, and the cradling shore.
God it was who let them die
filled with late understanding,
so who dares say we the innocent lurk
unpunished in the works and days?

FAMINE

The granary of heaven can never be full.
             — from a traditional Yoruba song

for Brian Hooper

The cow pales with meat,
bellies like a sail
the harvest blows.

The cow pales with hunger
like worn cloth
flapping pins of light.

Joseph plotted with weather
and pharaoh to save a people
on hunch and dream.

He knew what the chronicler didn't:
that the 7 years of one coincide
with the 7 years of the other.

Or who could dream that God's
lucidity could be held
in the baskets of caution?

Hunger marries plenty.
How God yearned to be felt
in the pang as in the full purse.

This Joseph knew —
Gold is the mirror
a lost heart earns.

In it behold feast's river
emptying into sea's oblivion.
Time is a place.

The native asks: This Egypt, must I love it
famished as when it golden stood?
Belonging is a reflex.

The exile says: Egypt full, a perfumed tide.
Empty, she is my child. Sand mocks grain
only when there is no bread.

When the granary's full,
the two musics rhyme,
their glass songs sharpen the sun.

I came upon this land as a child
yet sire enough of need
to know the difference between journey

and flight. And I came to love
Egypt, knowing beaten soil
and the deaf whip.

The man now from what was
cannot tell you what he loves more —
the sand, the grain, the obelisks

caught in dabs of onyx and silver
on the Nile's impatient flow,
or that Egypt fed as it hungered.

TITIAN'S DANAE

for Richard Wilbur

It is the same gold,
blushing out of the same veil
of cloud — neither chaos
nor storm nor the punctuations
of the horizon.
This cloud is the third party.
How different the eyes
that ponder the thump
and twinkle onto lap and velvet
of its aureate gush.
The muscular peasant woman,
too shabby to be a servant,
contrasts with the supple
yet masculine nude
young female, her head
drugged back
into the cupped palm
of the pillow
in the room her father sealed
against temptations.
These women are two desires
who have met here
to meet the painter's need
for stones at opposite
bases of an arch.
And the god so bent
on becoming when in lust
things other than a man,
has run out of beast
semblances, or bored of them,
has for once let himself

too become an object
of desire. The girl's
dropped head sighs a gaze
of misplaced gratitude,
like that which amens
requited prayers.
In a heavy doze she'll slip
into the shower of dream
and wait for it to change.
The old woman
is bark angry at herself
for not having brought
a deeper firmer apron
in which to belly the coinage
of divinity. She had never
stopped dreaming
of this moment,
when life would give
more than she could hold.
She is startled and bright.
This is no time to blur
into surfeit. Gather
or, as the lap dog,
snore into a furry loop
until the living passes.

II: WITHIN

FOUR

after Zurbarán's Still Life

*There are three things which are too wonderful for me, four which I do
not understand.*
        — *Proverbs 30 :18*

It was toward music the daring eye first lunged,
not knowing what otherwise to make
of this staged world in which the limelight
fell in turns on but one actor, thing, or thought.

At first is was the tent of sentence that nudged
the mind to ape the juggler's blur and loom.
Words like spinning fruit a circled ribbon
made, but the coup de sense left the jealous ear out.

Confuse the textured rub of meant sounds
with music, and prod the hunger for harmonies.
The eye knew at once: Remove procession
and one must take in time and journey at once.

No tear of peaks, no march of shields
can rival the sweep of this, the fist of now
that various vessels among themselves
shape deeply in the mind's place for sense.

SEVEN

after Bosch

Admittedly, they'll kill what only life can give,
that faded haunting from another time which then
we generously called the soul, but in reality

we'd rather think the engine fueled by gene or pain,
that animates act and wish. The sins petal
about the languid torso of a nude redeemer, wading

stiff in baptismal tides. Four scenes,
in circles too, square the central disk whose fables
teach and ridicule the beckoning conditions

of every life. Who hasn't played the lover torn with rage,
or hope a little profit comes from great respect?
Who wouldn't rather sleep the morning mass away

or sink so vainly warm in the sweet mirror's lake?
Never usher me from the splendid table,
nor find me, pray, leering at another's take.

But if you part the velvet drape of this our tent,
delight at least in the ventral dorsal heave within
where body does the spirit's chore and plays its harp.

And as for those other coins, each one describes
death and judgment and the worlds beyond,
where rhythmed pain too loves a bare bottom,

and angels, bored meticulous, kneel in air
and ready their horns to let the slumbered dead regain
that precious vase of flesh, no matter if in heaven.

IMMIGRANT PARABLE: HONG KONG ORCHID TREE, ARGUMENTS

> *Things stand outside our door, themselves by themselves, neither knowing nor reporting anything about themselves. What then does report about them? The governing self.*
> — *Marcus Aurelius, Book IX, art.15*

for Ann Rose

-I-

Like most trees that spend
their gorgeous efforts
on flowering, these have bitten
leaves and stripped twigs
that cling to branches and whip,
and mold-embroidered trunks.
They rise above perennial beds
of seedless refuse where vermin thrive
until the wind scatters the dead rattling.
It lifts the sunless dirt that haloed
the roots where once grass sprung.
How unnatural, too, these trees,
foreign and dragged onto this soil
to decorate at first, but soon to crowd
flora millennial weathers had tuned
like invisible violins. How they bully
the canopies, tangle the phone lines
and refuse to feed the venerable jay
and the citizen oriole.
Even their blooms are like the orchid
but cannot root in air and moisture
nor hold the branches harmless,
nor perfume the shade with hormonal fevers.
Behold how orchids paint their borrowed corners

with strokes of lust, but how these lumberings
breach sidewalk and plumbing
and will not a single true orchid host.
I doubt it is by nature's law —
more the force that keeps the real
from the imagined, and both from the mask.

-2-

It sturdied the wilting ground and shaded
the fly-strewn air. It spread in exponents
like a rhyme foretold by its doubling leaves,
and so it breathed geometry and pinned
its violet petals where only grasses grew,
the spiked palmetto, and the bleeding sandspur.
Unlike the melaleuca, it left untouched
water's balancing of earth and did not forget
the riding lessons of the typhoon.
Observe the more abundant bee and hummingbird,
the plentiful jars that grace the humblest sills,
the lovers who gather its sighs, and the oils
that emblem the painted tree for the place.
It bore beauty and magnitude onto a flat
murky plain and it unveiled
the languid shapely orchid where none here bloomed.
All its splendid brethren too are new —
hibiscus and haleconia, bougainvillea and bamboo.
It vies with araguaney for the bannering joys
but slips into half-naked sleep when poinciana
bursts into annual flame. It braves the fungus
and the termite and the saw. It knows its function
is to become the object of admired mistrust.

DUALISM PARABLE: PALM TREE, ARGUMENTS

La vida es el amor. Donde hay amores
Del tibio sol y arábigas arenas,
Hasta al desierto mismo nacen flores
Con palmas leves de murmullo llenas.
— José Martí, *Haschisch**

-I-

With neither tilt nor arc will you delude
those who know you are symmetry's
acolyte. The perfect rings from which once
huge leaves sprung, and the thin lift
of your insistent crown, mock
the branched multiform of other trees,
the globed heaviness of their canopies.
You, whose leaves are largest,
concentrate the heady swirl making
of royal straight and coconut bend
the emblems of posture. Behold the chaguaramo
guarding air and sun, marching down
the Ephesian-columned, Karnak-shaded avenue.
The girlish waist of christmas palm
and palmetto's armored mangle fill
the scene you've staged.
The simplest and the oldest tree
who heired the fern but preached the trunk,
stands yet in the familiar halfways
between flesh and flora. You are the point
on which the needle turns, yet we find
more mirror in oak, pear, and banyan
who herald our sculpture of thought
while you vent the heart

that shuts or wanes or bite-clings
like a fisted rag in the wind.

-2-

Indeed, the leafy twig, the brambled scope
of all that verdant barked enrapture
sailing up with breeze or toppling
trunk and all, trailing like a parachute
on the ground behind the diver's corpse —
indeed such trees do bring us to ourselves.
They do remind, instill, reflect — they are
the very verbs of our condition in leaf
enshrined. But the palm in its myriad single
forms, not whipped in arabesques
like the cypress yet fired to ear by the wind,
is the very stamp of sex, prime avenue
to sky, then piercing the ecstatic cloud,
geyser obelisk. Keep your frantic multiples
of heart and mind, tie them to the oak, the pear,
the willow, and the ficus. Mire them
like moth and the fly in webs
that from those branches the spider's hung
to catch the night and your higher rumblings.
Below, where the earth is, the palm
will not allow unambiguous instinct
to go unsigned. One-syllable tree,
the sigh, the fire palm.

> *Life is love. Where there are loves
> between the tepid sun and Arabian sands,
> even from the desert are flowers born
> and lithe palms filled with murmur.
> — José Martí, Hashish

38

CELLOPHANE, MARLBORO LIGHTS

Obedient to optics,
the transparent box will not,
like water, bend a shape
that enters it. It is not,
simply put, a translator.

Merely a pane that is
a box that is a skin.
Truly as light as smoke
to the eye,
nearly so to the nose,
less so to the fingertips,
and even less to the ear,
that third nose.

Tobacco shrapnel
comes to rest on the floor
of the box, the hand's pool.
Already the tiny fragrances
have grown into an identity.
As for us, it is a matter
of signal additions. We too
sum up into the vice
of familiars.

Now and then
the hurled chessboard
of recollections forces a regrouping.
The old self forms in thin air
like winter breath, says goodbye.
After the flood
the world knew itself only
by scent.

CONJURING BEAR

Morgan Falls, near Marquette, Upper Peninsula Michigan

Common deer and raccoon sightings spent,
I expect more. "The bear appear," says Duane,
my wilderness guide, "when we talk about them."
After three waterfalls and creeks boiling
over a harem of reclining boulders,
fallen tree trunks like calligraphied strokes
dominate the scroll of nature. We are
Buddhists by necessity. Amid the late spring
cedar twigs Duane breaks off, crumples, and orders
me "Smell this," the mind cannot hunt
for its usual pinings. It slips as do my urban feet
— why, I'm dancing on this creaky log —
holding obese steady with a branch;
I am a gondolier in a steamer's wake,
a drunken circus bear long accustomed
to the ruffled collar and the lash.
Duane possesses these woods,
and is in turn, by dint of patient gaze
and hunt. He snaps his relentless lens
at my precarious fording,
laughs to himself that such dare
faces off with inches of icy flow
that barely a pebble move.
He who stalked the full buck
of winter last across drifts
piled by lake winds — enough
to make even Duane an alien here.
And in the silence he shared
with the clearing and the beast
that halted there and turned
to look at him, he killed

and bound it, and slid
with it the decline to his truck
where rope and plank
held the buck's glass stare
tight against the rattling road home.
And the balance of the felling
was more than bodily —
took the taking of a man's heart
and lining it against the rigors
of winter. The beast that fed
all summer met that futility
in its random clearing pause.
Why struggle, why hope
to bridge one season with another,
stitching the daily canticles
into a taut drum. Once goat,
sheep or deer, now vessels
by whose beat we take,
kill, love, know.

QUILT COMPLEX

for Alisa Hummell

The beautiful names
for the patterns and ties
that bulging delicacy makes
are soon forgotten —
and that is the mark
of a marauding taste
like mine, an eye locked
in the tactile, fingertips
as second fiddles.
The woman who sewed it
had the lover's nervous handle
on the object of passion
which is always a process solidified —
simplicity as multiplication.
Patches annotate how light,
brick, bark, and wave
are herded, molten
into fabric concerti.
Sunset, building, tree, and lake —
themselves composed —
gather into theater.
I imagine clutching this familiar
curtain, bundling beneath it
in the fray and cure of sleep.
Not beneath, within
the field of the quilt
in its quartet of cleared,
plowed, fallow, and growing —
like a plane's view of farms unfurled.
Guardian land, skin of sleep,
I sink under this scape

bound from residual cloths.
Not for me, passing buyer
insisting on beauty and price.
But for children and husband
whom labor and winter
broke, strengthened.
I will frame these fields of holding
not having earned their kneaded warmth,
dwelling only on all
the rhythmed attributes of art
and hoping admiration will be
the better part of intrusion.

SAMURAI

Bruno came up to the girl at the bar
and she was already talking halfway
out of one side of her mouth while, he knew it,
looking at him with one eye at least through the smoke
she dropped everywhere from the chatted cigarette
and the pointed nails, and he knew it was all falling
in place, the look, the lights, the small moves he was
making toward her, the glance this way and that,
and when she said ham on rye to the waiter
he jumped in talking about samurai figuring
that was her thing, her lust right out of history,
dazed her a bit but she kept up her order ignoring
in that flirtatious opposite-of-what-I-really-want
kind of way his prize prey always gave him
despite his more and more on the sword, the layered
steel and the funny knobs of hair that meant all sorts
of things to heroes from back then and look simply
weird to her, no doubt, right? he asked, but I know
better, ham on rye came right by him and he stared
at it as she began to munch it trying harder to ignore
him, and then he finally broke down, Know
all about ham and rye, breed the pig, plough the field,
know all I need to know to get to that chewing.

SWINGLINE

A burglar noise below
and the right fist makes
for the grey steel stapler.

Hours of years in punched rites
have not erased this moment's duty
from the newly christened weapon.

To bludgeon, the object must ignore
its daily virtues, the useless line
of dual teeth it eggs within.

Like hushed Greeks in epic wood,
hoping to emerge in stealth
to undo a vaunted enemy.

It is the heavy form
and not the content which the moment
asks of the thing

traveling with the fist
across the dim house swaying,
down the muted steps,

into the den's promised
battle, where a shadow bends
over a filling bag.

The enemy vanishes
as the eyes close the dream.
He will come again

to change the nature of use.
A night will be when we'll both decide
who will bury himself in another's tale.

WINTER LANDSCAPE WITH A BIRD TRAP

after Bruegel

Not all the birds think the kernels
above the stick-propped board
are the gift of heaven. Some spy
and dawdle on the barren twigs
the season has knitted.
Like melted cages, the branches cannot hold,
yet the ambition is there.
As in the ice that so wants to burst
into warmth and drown
the paunchy mother with her wrapped child,
the skaters swinging sticks, the ambling villagers —
all caught in the hungers, minutes, and pennies.

And the bundling snow too wants its kill,
to take these talky mammals down
like the thin wolf or the late-born fawn.
All the forces of the wild will not shear
the species that hides in skins and houses.
Indeed, they've burnt down
nature's clock and storage
and war on borrowed soil. By mine
and net they balance the world
into purpose. And now a clever one

props a board up, drops corn and waits
for the birds to lose the fear
that brought them through the sun
green talon and claw. To fall
now under blight's sagacious shadow
in this parody of shelter, this house

the kind master must have built just for them —
the artless few who stayed the acrid season.

Was it wrong to hope for dropped petals of food
and a slice of roof to warm the ground?
And wrong to take the string that arcs
in the bitten gusts for the summer rope
a blur of children jump through?

Who but the safe dark starling
staring at the loose finches and sparrows
cradling into the trap could damn
their needs? Did he not scoff
at the scarecrow to crown his beak with corn
when all the harvester could do was hope
he'd had his fill? Starling's kin holds the string,
the brother featherless wing that shuts the trap.
The grim window is nature, too.

FLIGHT TO NASHVILLE

for Marta and James

There is no confusing
the cities at night beneath us
for lava or nebulae,
although they rhyme
with tentacles drawn
against an ocean's concrete night.

How prey and predator
must farm upon themselves
bacteria to harvest their glow —
surest kin to our static lace
of settlement, the cordoned fire
and the glinted maze.

Night's our punctual depth,
yet only the flotsam eyes
can see what blazes
the cradling village brought us to.
When the anthracite spaces
were grazed by the hearth's poor reach

all of life, all earth
quarried the mind for winged fears
and signed its scourings with ash and ember.
Now we, herded in numberless arks,
are the vulgar gods, bulging
in cramped seats, imagining

populations dozing in the grids
of bright shell habitats — these towns,
abacus and spill, streets like nerves

lightning toward stadia and malls.
We name them and live them,
and turn them into deepest denizens
simply by looking out the window.
Land's the sea vantage has proclaimed.
We are needles eyeing a compass, arcing
the tidal voids for trifling warmths
and forgotten prayers. To those below
we are a moving star too slow for wishes.

III: ROUND

FLYING OVER THE BAHAMAS

Undecided matter, oil fulgent,
pages dissolving, gelling,
fluttering in a turquoise breeze.

Height opals life,
reduces it to vastness,
yet, yearning for particulars,

these premonitions of land
darken the sea in shapes
of what gathers there —

the manta's sweep, the fin
or tail, all projects of form
a tide has shuffled and lain down.

A speck of village or a crack of road
assumes artifice but cannot claim
the nimbus-mottled estuaries

nor the rivers the surf has etched
upon the landless sand. The veilings halt
when a field of pale green disks bloom —

a crown of saline arenas
signing what rose or pooled
from the agents of the earth.

Residual halos of boiled escapes,
they imitate the marks of drops
as if surface met all impacts

with the same imprint. This is how
nature's words are formed,
to turn these shift of islands

into a liquid moon whose dips
and phased shadows remind
what light owes to the laws of murk.

FLIGHT TO L.A.

Not till Abilene did the clouds break
that hid for three and a half hours
Florida and the Gulf, and the delta
I had once observed materialize
for thirty minutes from murk
and dying sea into the flesh of land.
The continent has shifted in unseen hues
beneath clouds that looked like snow
tracked by boot, bike and truck.
But now with the land rising
and the badlands unfamiliar with the dank
corpuscular white that quilts the heavens
above sea and farm, I see the pumice blues
whose mix with ochers and greys
make the desert plain. And terrible.
Who could help imagine miner and outlaw,
migrant or soldier lost in such a place —
a patch of which from here could sink
hope and fortitude in the swirled dust
of riverbed or the cratered shell of lake.
Yet the land beckoned, and beckons.
Here and there the glint of some human
planting of steel, a rooftop or a car hood,
echoes the marches thirsty for gold
or the tribes who tamed the savage
residues of naked sun
and forged the intimate cistern.
Whether by shards of light, armied demarcations,
or the mounting poise of approaching city,
we are the beast who do more than leave
our bones on the fiery earth.

And we alone can lower the blind upon it
as the clouds come gather again to shut
our sights and cool the urgent ground.

HUNTERS IN THE SNOW

after Bruegel

From and toward the bitter white
they trudge, down the breasted slope
to the angled squares of roofs
and the green banners of stiff ponds
dotted with skaters. The hunters
are like the bonfire at the inn's door,
of that proud element, and not the fluid
cracked by season or the air that lets
a scissors of a bird turn and dip.

Where is the earth? The gaunt dogs sniff for it,
the trees are anchored in it, absent beneath
the fallen season that has skirted and drowned
the tired ground. All that fruit and grain,
all the trembling shades. This is the time
to shut away and let men find the world
without it. Let them think they feel
the ground beneath the anvil of boot.
They know the brown black trees
are its ripped streamers.

Finally, hulked and gunned, and ready
for tavern and whore, they swell to know
they are earth. But in the coughed vapors,
they are the air too. In sweat, piss and spittle,
the water. All four elements reel within them —
beast but master.

And something else, not the shot soul
but what the baked village so daintily speaks.
The dwellers gather, yet they dot distances

that cannot reduce mountain or the flood grey
of sky. Even the village is too small to be noticed
by the soaring bird. Yet what else returns home
marked by its choice of bloods? What else can live
by a hugged prayer or count the small change of hope?
What else can draw blazes from the snow
or dance upon the diamond ponds?

IBISES, MIAMI

They are too large for the tangling city scene,
the dusty roar, the trash, blares, and edges
of its speeds. And yet they alight serene

on median strips and bank lawns, the richest
beast in view. Asian ballerina balanced
to strike a lizard in the reeds. Just

to feed the tight white frame and dance
in that slow motion garners praise,
but ibis also aims to startle remembrance

with simpler feats. Behold the art by which they raise
their necks to pluck then loop to preen
and how, while gardeners mow and yawn, they poise

their fan wings on a hedge and weave their lean
legs and talons like tendrils on a branch.
They watch the ruckus of world with an eye as keen

as any other bird's, but when they launch
to flight it is not in fear but sadly sure
their act has not a single sigh procured.
Art's awkward duty is to ask too much.

THE RICE BIRD

Sister Robert of the fifth grade assigned us
to make an image of a bird by glueing
colored rice to a board. Holding little

art, and always having rice for dinner,
I could not think but ask my mother's friend,
the neighbor downstairs, to help me.

A bird made of rice, she sighed. Without a yes,
we dove into her kitchen. I watched her
first explain how it might take shape

on the board, then give up the teaching
to devour the task herself, talking to herself
as she glued the dyed grains on her sketch.

A mosaic oriole or jay, except the colors
had gone to that side of nature nature ignored —
the fervent phoenix and the aureate dove.

The bird was perched on a branch
that trembled in her memory alone,
And now, she said giving me

a creature byzantine with light
and pointillist drunk, Take this bird
to your teacher. I was dumb,

not knowing if I should take credit
for what I had not created. Guessing this,
she said as if opening a cage door,

Now when you buy a canary you say it's yours
though it is God's. Simpler, then, to assume
this boon from a neighbor, this gift of rice.

SEVEN MILE BRIDGE, FLORIDA KEYS

For one mile of it or thereabouts a pelican
flew beside us, glided exactly above
the concrete wall of the bridge, barely
a feather or muscle moving, exact
as a line thrown on the page of the world
with a ruler. From a quarter mile back
I saw the bird lift syrup slow, then suddenly
aright itself and take to an invisible
track four feet or so above the barrier,
and I knew I would have to brake a bit, and more
as we got closer, to cruise along his glide
in that joy exclusive to parallels.
Never mind that we were coming home
from a honeymoon, and that any dicethrow
of weather, bloom, sand, cloud, any dicethrow
spoke utterly of harmonies. Never mind love.
We, axle-bound and land-held, got to glide
along with Icarus, red-striped chest, grey and white,
thick as purpose, as if designed for nothing
if not for this trajectory, this one flight
to escort the poetry of coincidences.

RUBENS: DANCE OF THE VILLAGERS

Sixteen dancers and a flutist in a tree
flanked by the surge of green, the fine
house to the right where the village crests,
all the rest of it hid, except a wall or two
halting by the canvas edge, no breeze.

Is it clear they dance? Could they be
refugees, hands clasped as children do
when afraid? Or broken troops, or hunters
moving on their prey? What attention
do they pay, that of task or pleasure?

Perhaps at stake is how mist and farm
vanish, stacked against the spiraling
mass of peasants loose in the artist's eye,
motion against distance disguised
as people braided by feeling.

But the lone flutist affirms it is a dance,
as do the bare toes fanning on the grass,
for why else would the girl in blue
not stop to tuck her left breast
back in her dress? And why is the one

in red prepared to make such tangled chore
of a kiss? Why is everyone keeling
and soared to the brink? If not dance
why the pairs, and why the kerchief
bridge the others must dip beneath

as if the music told them to? What it commands
is the step and bounce, for bodies
are ears when man and woman face

with nothing but music between them,
and what's left of a day's clothes, and fields.

But it's the flutist who upholds the dance, sun
to the sixteen who counter the clocks of youth,
tip and, yes, they are laughing, and each
has one hand of two mates in a chain
of twirl and kick as the wind and the flute rise.

OFFSHORE ISLAND, FLORIDA KEYS

To the west a clump of green above the turquoise
and lavender water, a wall were it not mounded, long
and of the same height almost its whole length,
bricked with the same kind of leaves,
mangrove or seagrape or some other thick kind,
hardly a branch showing, and uniformly verdant
were it not for a seeming random hail of white
spots, two dozen a glance counts, and driving
fast they look like rags a botanist might have tied,
or markers left by some agriculture department
guy measuring the spread of flies or fungi,
but they are ibises at rest, fruit heavy,
and like them harvest patient, and were it not
for one large bird alighting in flutters,
then turning into one more dab
of snow against green against turquoise,
blue, and violet, swallowed into home,
I would have never known.

THE GOOD EARTH, THE GOOD STARS

after Whitman

Esse est percipi
                    — *Berkeley*

In their tentatives, the single cells
lunge at the impossible star

numbers, splitting relentless
until the hope of constellation

blurs in the exponential jellies
of astronaut skies.

The blue green living slide.
To what eye might the amoeba

and the plankton be stars?
What knows them slow enough

to guide, if not Distance?
Cementer of course, you make

the panicked lights quiet
in the earthly eye, so that together

in the basket of young night, we love
and ponder the sky as embedded stillness.

Distance, you have given us
the intimate models of speed

and tumult. You parted the curtain
on analogies, as when Galileo

trained the loop of planets
like horse-drawn coaches racing.

The gain, falling back, gain once more
of two bodies in motion shocked

away the earth-centered orbits
first in thought, then with lens.

So many bursting shells and splitting nuclei,
the world cannot hold still and be one world,

rather like a lung infinitely inhaling,
it surges with addition. The opposite

would be lovers hinged onto one another,
closing the plane of one world's page

onto another. The opposite of the world
is union, fertility's overture.

The world cannot love
because its flesh is number.

SEA FORMS

after Dale Chihuly

It was not enough to ape the sea,
the twinge of kelp, the tossed anemone,
but to find it in the flesh of glass.

Nor to seek the trumpet free of brass
among the dented cones and bitten shells
for here the music drowns in cobalt swells

and no ear lurks. It was the ocean
that lit itself in slow formation,
that left its coils and ripples and retreats

and bent the wave and edged its pleats
with opal whisperings of hue.
It was the ocean that lent its blue

to bowl and the conch remembrance
because it heard of art's endurance
and had had enough of wave and salt,

the hearty rhetoric of what cannot halt
at the brink. The sea yearned for signature
but knew indelibility outside its nature

would defraud. Behold its stiff spalsh
in painted oils, on film its vapid flash,
and never mind the frittered torn of words

in poems that cannot concoct, or worse
exploit its rhythmed restlessness.
And so it brought to the curled gem of glass

its burn to imprint its soul. Let air
blow on fiery sand and so repair
the time-scarred, inconsolable sea.

BOGOTÁ, BARRIO NORTE

for Olga and Jim Amaral

Tudor and brick frame the frame
around this courtyard chilled
with rose, cherry, and fuschia.
The scenting vines soften
the high brick and pointed gates,
and the thin sun crumpling now
has tracked the air
with a lowered cloud. I breathe

safe and balconied until a siren
nears then halts then lets
a single note blare weaker
in distances the pauses made.
What civil war hasn't sundered
gets ready for the theater, the café,
or slouches before the dozing news.

Rome too, long lived past herself,
must have spun the days and chores,
tedious, litigious, laughing and otherwise
heaped on the adjectives of the quotidian.
Regardless is a city. Who can dread
the Hun in Gaul or the Goth in Spain
where the columns shade the gurgling
font, and the garden flickers malarial
in the silk narcotic of the rose.

A STUDENT LAMENTS KNOWING TOO MUCH MUSIC HAS RUINED HIS LOVE OF WHAT'S ON THE RADIO

The once thrilled chords now rubble into noise,
the then felt, the ertswhile related real,

have fled like zoo beasts in a hurricane
that cracked the vaults and drenched the locks.

No growl or coo will bring them back,
feather screached and hairy backed,

for inmates of instinct and appetite
know there's but one dark forest —

oblivion, happily. He turns the knob clockwise
on his deaf radio and watches

the red bar slide like the edge
of a shutting prison door, then counters to open

it again as if he were the universal warden
somber now that all pleasures have climbed away

and cut the wires and joined the vanished free.
His mind yearns for fill. Return, baby heart, return

to the shock of garden, cupped in stone. We were
happiest when we did not know feeling's timbre

was best just so. We ate the served meal, tasted
good so we called it a hunt. O baby, baby, come home.

IMAGING SNOW

Marquette, Michigan

for John Smolens

June 15th, still light at 10 PM,
the sun at last subtropical sets
later every day. "Last winter
we were 8 inches shy of our own record,"
has been the daily chant from natives
for the last two weeks. Yesterday
the mercury hit 95 degrees
only to have a brief shower
melt it down to 65 by evening.
Ignoring the thermometer,
the locals don sandals and shorts
for it is their time. Everyone
takes stock of the bank
digital temperature reading —
a flashing screen on every corner.
The lights by which these thermals
are proclaimed form the starwork
by which lives navigate, labors
migrate from snow shovel to trowel.

A visiting Miamian, I revel in my June sweater,
dally among poppies, petunias, irises
and tulips. A breeze crumples
the deciduous trees into foil,
and birds shake out of them
like change from trousers — robins,
jays, sparrows — like those back home.
And the swaggering gulls on the ground,
more thuggish here, cry like crowbars

wedging the doors, ripping into sky blue
garbage bags to strew their bounty
like stolen cash down the neat streets.
Tissue and wet labels mock
the ice that clung to grass through May.
The natives are consummate peaceful.
Never a door locked. Cars in winter
are left running curbside while shoppers
dawdle over the right cantaloupe.

Yet I am not square with the place.
Our summers halt at the airconditioned door,
and usually the hurricane's swung ax
misses. But here the drifts will come,
erect their Trojan ramparts
around every frail house, tunnel
the streets. Then the season's meager
sun will blind the novice snow.
And the merry tales that now in warmth
abound will anchor in this emblem time:
the woman who can only
enter and leave her home
through the second story window,
the April blizzard that erased
the teasing thaw, the famished deer
men hunt in ravenous mercy,
the snap of power line,
the vanished runway.

I recall myself marooned by war
in Canada, when not even youth
could coax a sleave of warmth
from the mechanics of latitudes
and pressure that rule season.
When I too lived on winter's rail

I readied house and mind
the hourglass summer long
and squinted down horizons
knowing the engine but a dot
whose order would soon
roll upon and through.
Then too I'd see the iris and the tulip
as welcome insolents, and my pupils
widened as lakes
resumed their liquid jostle.

Now I visit among the celebrants
of the new sun but reject
the lessons of treasuring
home's unchecked fertility.
I claim the artless luxury of awe
at these folk who bury two thirds
of their year and make
of summer flesh and not a time.
My arms chill with another poplar gust
that rattles leaves like shell bits
on a beach the always Gulfstream
warmth tosses like popcorn.
I am cold here, but they are natural
who sip prodigious green like wine.

IV: ABOUT

Clean as meat cut by a cleaver,
the concrete edifice sponges up the halogen
beams. The polite lamps hide
in beds of river-washed stones
and beneath the flowering shrubs.
Pinned-tie neat and scrubbed,
the building is too new to be noticed,
though it could hangar a couple
of Parthenons or that Roman shell
ablaze in Baalbek reds
that stands in books filled with ruins.
The senses alone do not make awe happen,
to the garage's spectacular loss.
The marble-stripped, bullet-pocked,
weather-emblazoned wall, brick, and shard
are the eye's inverted sirens, wrecked
and of song long emptied.
 Scar trains the will — makes the carcass live
in the reverential mind.

OPENINGS

> *In memoriam: Eduardo Chibás, fiery Cuban political activist against government corruption in the forties, founder of the Ortodoxo Party; committed suicide August 5, 1951.*

The flood shares the vanity of all
preambles. Whether it mounts

in drizzles, then torrents, then pools
that have nowhere to go but up,

past wall and sandbag, into air
it can never possess,

Babel-sure and Phrixus-dizzy,
whirling, tipping the hat of roof

until the waters waffle drunk lying
across erstwhile rock austerities

like cushions in a dim harem.
Or whether it walls offshore

defiant of laws and sense,
like the hair's anger or the hunt

have risen, and rising thus
shadow the merciless land

before dropping its jaw upon it
blind to flight and deaf to prayer

and, though gleaming, mirrors nothing.
Even the softest kiss, the morsel

that opens the novel of obesity,
or the first purchase beyond reach —

all overtures betray their assigned role
as harbingers. They are, in fact, islands

of closure. They cease the world before
but only point to themselves. Adhere

to their cold, meticulous eye. See it
in the olive soldiers that came down

from mountains promising freedom.
All Havana then tossed in preemptive carnival,

sacking itself of measure and purpose.
Nothing could hold back the fall

 — not principle of struggle,
not the burial of Cuba's Baptist

eight years before. Who calls in the flood
if not the flood? The first summary trials

applauded, the firing squads cheered.
And the lead of destiny molten folded

into the hollows, inhaling itself
into the dorsal sails. But unlike the flood

it would not recede. This was one beginning
that would brook no end.

PARABLE HUNTER

-I-

Miami's only mystery is the banyan tree.
Beneath a canopy that clouds a city block

spreads the sunless ink of its reign.
There shall be no grass in its dominion.

In place of a trunk a twisting smoke of branches,
their vines hardening into grey pillars

once they've reached the destined earth.
The strangler's kin, flora's answer

to nebulae and empire, it thickens
by tentacle turning into branch, swirls

gelled in the amber of growth, recalling
the marble hands of that nymph almost

caught in flesh by reason and music
but without lust, chase, or lamentation.

In its Bengal home, the banyan has sprawled
into reverence. Here it mounds toward heaven

above golfers and, further off, joggers and walkers.
Fifteen vegetable monuments, red-berried

green cumuli forged together, raining
their dark matter to the ground, quiet

as mountains yet herd-like — a still shot
of dinosaurs above sightless ferns.

Tiny golfers smoke and chat about their rim,
scattered like dropped coins

on the regulation green, its shades shifting
like an estuary in failing light.

-2-

How can our soft ground hold these trees?
Sand and sponge and the brittle coral

mangrove and developer have beaten
into territory that deserts, in hurricanes,

the ficus and the oak, the royal and the coconut palm.
This ground mushes in one day of steady rain, sinks

car and golfer into murk. Yet the banyans
have mastered the arguments of weight

enough to stand their ground and citadel
the flocks of egress, the swarms of duty.

Banyan's triumph makes the god-maker's sense
clear, for surely they have been hewn from air

and it must be a god of that that nestles there.
And if so, what kindred power made the mud

or taught it to refuse to drink the season?
Well, the god of chance or the god of art,

for the world is mud upon which all steps leave
their prints but few do fossils make.

Will only keep some privy specimen to show
what voyagers once were, but not their journeys.

-3-

In central India above the banyan's head there is a cliff
where men a thousand years ago carved thirty-four

temples out of stone, out of the belly of stone.
Shiva, Buddha, Arihanta spin in a necklace

of shrine and sanctuary. The gods of the place
slept, danced, and braided the pilgrims' steps

toward them like fronds of incense milking the air.
Chamber and the golden hums of meditation

raised stupa and icon, pillar and path.
The real chant of the place is divine

insculptability that beckons the chisel
and the brush, the robe and beaten feet.

We orbit and that is all we know;
the metaphors of proximity bind us

to solemn distances. But metaphor we must,
carving, swinging, praying, writing, living

into the granite and the tender green, holding sway
over the difficult ground, bracing for wind.

SALT

The movies always show the wave
leaping off the rocks, off the very sea
onto Havana's malecón.

Cheap currency: wave as desire.
The sea cannot hold still
when the land shakes its skirts.

And everywhere salt paints
pavement and crack, the steps
of lovers and tourists, boys

hoping the sea is not what it seems.
20's buildings whose cement was mixed
with dredged sand learn to crumble

in obedience to matter. Like the waves,
salt reaches beyond its tempering,
devours what it silently once upheld.

No one could have stormed the possibility
of salt as clock, the inner appetite
of substance against substance.

Like wages, then, and the arena,
salt embitters the tongue that courses
the world. It cannot see itself

in its word progenies. Known as youth,
salt begs for tastes, for the ordinance
to slay familiars. Here, in Havana

it will raise the earth, lift it like a wave
up to the prayer-stricken clouds.
The boys do not want the shell bits

embedded in the old concrete to steal
the wonder of a beach risen like a page,
defying the ocean it once possessed.

POLYSEMIA AND ARITHMETIC WHILE WALKING THE DOG

Penetrad sin temor, memorias mías,
Por donde ya el verdugo de los días
Con igual pie dio pasos desiguales.
              — Luís de Góngora y Argote, *A la memoria de la*
muerte y el infierno (1612)*

In the single bark of a word, shelves
of values gather. "Trunk" — the mind deals —

and boxers and elephants converge,
torso and chest. And trees

which Lacho's nose inspects
for every nipple of nuance,

as Father Narciso did with a sonnet
by Góngora in the tenth grade

while we dozed or shuffled anxiously
hoping the hour would seep faster.

For symmetry's sake, there should be
ten meanings for "trunk." Cheat a little — swimmer's

trunks, truncate — the total comes to 7.
Trunk line in communications, 8.

The trunk on a boat, that's 9.
Why not hoist aboard a trunk fish

for 10? It wouldn't take ten years
for Narciso to die, of a brain tumor.

I will soon be old enough to be his father.
But not for another street or two.

The leverage of words offers no symmetry.
Meaning is more like this walk.

A blur of blocks away from my house,
and situated in no angle from it

which the geometric mind might savor, we will come
onto that yellow house with the wild bushes

and the white frayed trim. A grey angora
near the walkway will see us approach

and sink into the deaf high grass
like a fat compass. In the backyard

a grey dog will howl the world around him
like a lasso, stand like a man against the chainlink fence.

Which meaning of "possess" takes this moment?
The cat's focused stealth conflates

the prep to pounce with hushed alert.
While the dog heralds too much,

and banners protest with clouds of soil.
It seems the poem's choice is the feline's

subterranean glow, all intention and poise.
But it cannot ignore the world's thick boister

and tangle, its axe of numbers. It took 35 years,
but now I understand the wisdom of water

trundling from marble thighs and words jarring
a lace of clauses: Only the baroque is clear.

> *Penetrate, without fear, memories of mine,*
> *Along the path which the executioner of days*
> *Has already tread with equal feet and unequal steps.*
> — Luís de Góngora y Argote, *A la memoria de la*
> *muerte y el infierno*

They seem to grow from their seats
like geraniums on a sill or heliotropes
facing the monitors, grazing the concave
with their fingertips, palms greened
then reddened and blued by the flux
of the game-tossed images. Their leaves
shift in the interlaced, hypnotic notes
of computerized slot machines.
No slots, arms, or spin of gears.
This is a tribal house surrounded
by wilderness minutes from the city.
The floor attendants' uniforms
pretend Miccosukee weavings,
and the door is guarded by a 1957 grey,
restored Thunderbird behind velvet ropes.
Inside, bingo and poker tables timidly skirt
the nebula of buzz and hum number ovens.
No roulette or blackjack. Convention
center halls chime with the serial music
of a thousand tubes sweeping
their bubbling knells into one held snore.

The ear's jackpot doesn't count.
Across the room a feeble siren
turns a red light atop a contraption,
heralding someone's win of something.
A handful of heads swivel momentarily
but swing back to join the Order
of the Fixed Stare, a flock statically plunging
into chosen games. They are the common
odds of the race, voter soldier rock of labor
on which the sighing Porch of Maidens stands,
the Gothic, Goya, and the Shinto shrine.

I want to think they are all ticks on a dead dog,
or rows of sweltering teats on its stiff belly.
I want the worst for the way my mind
shows them to their seats in my theater
of the place. I want to sneer,
as an innocent would a damning jury,
at their ridiculous hopes.
Beneath the mere ground
patient magma warms what it will sear.

Meanwhile I sip my drink at the Cypress Lounge
beneath the frills of a fake bamboo hut
and take a long drag from my allowed cigar.
No poem from their condition hails,
nor mine. Perhaps I could throw the false
promise of the Thunderbird against
the acidic clash of aquas, oranges and pinks
that wrench rather than decorate the eye's
having of the place. And call forth
the old cupped days of quarters
or the physical spin of the wheel
and the velvet feel of risk.
If history is breath,
we're in the shrink of exhale.
Nor is there exile in this script,
no sob to pillar the burning bridge.

But there is a prayer — growled, bitten.
O do not let the world become inexorably
this constant spiral down away
from pleasure and into the forged textures.
Force it by Your whim to be loyal
to what's been hewn from the daily cave
by millennia of aspirations.
Uphold what the feeling thinking few

have thrown off their leaden backs
and made to hawk hover.
Once the world gambled on imagining
and won. Do not permit
the pursuit of subtlety to die
in the lush drone of planted beings.
Do not, I beg, let numbers have their way.

RYMAN AUDITORIUM, NASHVILLE

You can tell the wind's intent
by which slope of the Ryman's roof
the pigeons are huddled upon.

A semicircle of fifty birds
hinged by the crest of roof —
in what was once a church and still believes

angles point to God. The flock signs
refuge on what was only shield,
and made the aegis into home.

Knowing they have turned
the sky into a room by clustering here,
and roof into a wall,

they cannot imagine another flock
completes their circle on the other slope,
for that would turn the roof

into a leaf, the spine into a vein,
and each decline into a barren mirror
that only will can tame into refraction.

Yet, by gathering so, the pigeons
conjure phantom kin that brave
the crowning chill, the spliced updraft,

and all the forces that erase inept talon
from grove and shingle. Farming
the windward, they roost still as eggs.

No, there is but one roof, one slant,
as there is one wind unborn and undying.
One sail to burn the air to stillness.

FIRE SERMON, MATACUMBE KEY

Passing them by, we say we'd love to own
a house on stilts by the rocky sea, facing
the bronze horizon of this ripe hour,
while training our eyes on Vacancy signs.
Long weekend, winter tourism. The Keys
are full, heavy as a muddy whip. The houses
are lit with new bulbs and festive familiars.
We can almost smell the roasting catch,
imagine hearing the atmospheric musics
and all the joyous catapults of mirth
hauled out on such family gatherings
to get the spirit right. It is winter and we can
almost forget why the homes rise above
garage level on concrete legs. In the summer
and fall the hurricanes come through and near,
and the narrow buckle of land melts
beneath the surge, the trees fly, the fish dash
against wall, driveway, lamp.
It is on these lofty planes
that the cherished cluster
as if by edict tide and moon.

Prison and pines to my left,
Lake Superior to my right,
I am driving toward Marquette
from Harvey, slumping
the slow hush of a hill's demise
when I glimpse the grey dome
and the two power plant stacks
that sign the town from a distance.
Around it is the dark green that fields
the torn banner of the peninsula.

A late spring fog has risen
from Superior and begun
to move upon the town.
Thick enough to catch some blue
and yellow but still affirm its pearl
condition, the fog is form
and the town but space scored
by the notes of rooftops.
It waits for the muscle of thought
to possess it, not as the opal of milk
paints the drunk glass, for idea fills
and hates the fraud of linger.
The fog is deafer than the town,
bears the mantle of patient harken.

It need not besiege,
merely breathe
itself into the cookie sheet
streets and the crisp houses.
Fog resists all stories, deplores
its compulsory giantism.
It would rather sit

the long day out
or rally with the failed night
of summer. It has not come
to make the place precious,
bewildered by the nature
that holds it so
like a fawn on a brittle
sandstone outcrop.
It will not rescue
by seeming to devour,
or spread the picnic of pity
on those whose eyes and lights
fail on the white.
It is in them, breathed into.
It is them, the music
of their wet cool throats.
Look at space, at air,
it says. Thought
has its flesh
from the hill
on the road from Harvey.

And you who are driving toward
my town — hums the fog —
on your desultory race
to see who enters it first.
You whose indigent weather
pattern of cigar smoke
in the cabin of that borrowed car
parodies the cell-wall to horizon
sweep of my presence, you
have one purpose.
Witness from strangeness
how I dwell.

BEAUFORT SCALE

The experts agree to guess and hint
the hurricane away from us. Yet, near enough,
will turn yard-size canopies into crafts

reeling in the sea. A void has stalled
in the Gulfstream, her breeze is firm
and her sky glares aluminum.

Clouds race in the direction the broadcast
says they must race. I walk the dog and review
my memories twelve years past of a storm

that didn't miss, and how I walked
the neighborhood then too, as if to shape
from the last familiars the tactics of yearning.

Now I do not stop to memorize what will
be gone by morning: that wooden house
framed by palm trees two doors down,

the orchid-drunk gazebo, or the spidery screen
hooding a neighbor's pool. In this storm branches
will tear and only the weakest trunks will fail,

but it might be days before the dog gets
a decent walk again. He sniffs the ledger
on a tree and adds his signature, pulls me deeper

beneath fertile years of ficus and orchid trees
roiling and bright with sudden gusts.
The Admiral's scale, once keyed to white sea

and ambrosial wind, rehearses the navigation
of this storm amid our vined and flowery scapes.
Precision turned his name into an adjective

for that is what every noun aspires to be.
The city that banners a wine or music,
a disease that claims origin and future at once

in a land no storm can rend from tales.
Admiral, your name numbers
the jostled branch and the bowling sail,

disclosing how numbers serve the restive mind
a summons to mate conditions with a name.
We turn home chilled by gusts in the dead of summer.

The Carnegie Mellon Poetry Series
Backlist 1990-2008

1990

Why the River Disappears, Marcia Southwick
Staying Up For Love, Leslie Adrienne Miller
Dreamer, Primus St. John

1991

Permanent Change, John Skoyles
Clackamas, Gary Gildner
Tall Stranger, Gillian Conoley
The Gathering of My Name, Cornelius Eady
A Dog in the Lifeboat, Joyce Peseroff
Raised Underground, Renate Wood
Divorce: A Romance, Paula Rankin

1992

Modern Ocean, James Harms
The Astonished Hours, Peter Cooley
You Won't Remember This, Michael Dennis Browne
Twenty Colors, Elizabeth Kirschner
First A Long Hesitation, Eve Shelnutt
Bountiful, Michael Waters
Blue for the Plough, Dara Wier
All That Heat in a Cold Sky, Elizabeth Libbey

1993

Trumpeter, Jeannine Savard
Cuba, Ricardo Pau-Llosa
The Night World and the Word Night, Franz Wright
The Book of Complaints, Richard Katrovas

1994

If Winter Come: Collected Poems, 1967–1992, Alvin Aubert
Of Desire and Disorder, Wayne Dodd
Ungodliness, Leslie Adrienne Miller
Rain, Henry Carlile
Windows, Jay Meek
A Handful of Bees, Dzvinia Orlowsky

1995

Germany, Caroline Finkelstein
Housekeeping in a Dream, Laura Kasischke
About Distance, Gregory Djanikian
Wind of the White Dresses, Mekeel McBride
Above the Tree Line, Kathy Mangan
In the Country of Elegies, T. Alan Broughton
Scenes from the Light Years, Anne C. Bromley
Quartet, Angela Ball
Rorschach Test, Franz Wright

1996

Back Roads, Patricia Henley
Dyer's Thistle, Peter Balakian
Beckon, Gillian Conoley
The Parable of Fire, James Reiss
Cold Pluto, Mary Ruefle
Orders of Affection, Arthur Smith
Colander, Michael McFee

1997

Growing Darkness, Growing Light, Jean Valentine
Selected Poems, 1965-1995, Michael Dennis Browne
Your Rightful Childhood: New and Selected Poems, Paula Rankin
Headlands: New and Selected Poems, Jay Meek
Soul Train, Allison Joseph
The Autobiography of a Jukebox, Cornelius Eady

The Patience of the Cloud Photographer, Elizabeth Holmes
Madly in Love, Aliki Barnstone
An Octave Above Thunder: New and Selected Poems, Carol Muske

1998

Yesterday Had a Man In It, Leslie Adrienne Miller
Definition of the Soul, John Skoyles
Dithyrambs, Richard Katrovas
Postal Routes, Elizabeth Kirschner
The Blue Salvages, Wayne Dodd
The Joy Addict, James Harms
Clemency and Other Poems, Colette Inez
Scattering the Ashes, Jeff Friedman
Sacred Conversations, Peter Cooley
Life Among the Trolls, Maura Stanton

1999

Justice, Caroline Finkelstein
Edge of House, Dzvinia Orlowsky
A Thousand Friends of Rain: New and Selected Poems, 1976-1998,
    Kim Stafford
The Devil's Child, Fleda Brown Jackson
World as Dictionary, Jesse Lee Kercheval
Vereda Tropical, Ricardo Pau-Llosa
The Museum of the Revolution, Angela Ball
Our Master Plan, Dara Wier

2000

Small Boat with Oars of Different Size, Thom Ward
Post Meridian, Mary Ruefle
Hierarchies of Rue, Roger Sauls
Constant Longing, Dennis Sampson
Mortal Education, Joyce Peseroff

How Things Are, James Richardson
Years Later, Gregory Djanikian
On the Waterbed They Sank to Their Own Levels, Sarah Rosenblatt
Blue Jesus, Jim Daniels
Winter Morning Walks: 100 Postcards to Jim Harrison, Ted Kooser

2001

The Deepest Part of the River, Mekeel McBride
The Origin of Green, T. Alan Broughton
Day Moon, Jon Anderson
Glacier Wine, Maura Stanton
Earthly, Michael McFee
Lovers in the Used World, Gillian Conoley
Sex Lives of the Poor and Obscure, David Schloss
Voyages in English, Dara Wier
Quarters, James Harms
Mastodon, 80% Complete, Jonathan Johnson
Ten Thousand Good Mornings, James Reiss
The World's Last Night, Margot Schilpp

2002

Among the Musk Ox People, Mary Ruefle
The Memphis Letters, Jay Meek
What it Wasn't, Laura Kasischke
The Finger Bone, Kevin Prufer
The Late World, Arthur Smith
Slow Risen Among the Smoke Trees, Elizabeth Kirschner
Keeping Time, Suzanne Cleary
Astronaut, Brian Henry

2003

Imitation of Life, Allison Joseph
A Place Made of Starlight, Peter Cooley
The Mastery Impulse, Ricardo Pau-Llosa
Except for One Obscene Brushstroke, Dzvinia Orlowsky

Taking Down the Angel, Jeff Friedman
Casino of the Sun, Jerry Williams
Trouble, Mary Baine Campbell
Lives of Water, John Hoppenthaler

2004

Freeways and Aqueducts, James Harms
Tristimania, Mary Ruefle
Prague Winter, Richard Katrovas
Venus Examines Her Breast, Maureen Seaton
Trains in Winter, Jay Meek
The Women Who Loved Elvis All Their Lives, Fleda Brown
The Chronic Liar Buys a Canary, Elizabeth Edwards
Various Orbits, Thom Ward

2005

Laws of My Nature, Margot Schilpp
Things I Can't Tell You, Michael Dennis Browne
Renovation, Jeffrey Thomson
Sleeping Woman, Herbert Scott
Blindsight, Carol Hamilton
Fallen from a Chariot, Kevin Prufer
Needlegrass, Dennis Sampson
Bent to the Earth, Blas Manuel De Luna

2006

Burn the Field, Amy Beeder
Dog Star Delicatessen: New and Selected Poems 1979-2006,
    Mekeel McBride
The Sadness of Others, Hayan Charara
A Grammar to Waking, Nancy Eimers
Shinemaster, Michael McFee
Eastern Mountain Time, Joyce Peseroff
Dragging the Lake, Robert Thomas

2007

So I Will Till the Ground, Gregory Djanikian
Trick Pear, Suzanne Cleary
Indeed I Was Pleased With the World, Mary Ruefle
On the Vanishing of Large Creatures, Susan Hutton
One Season Behind, Sarah Rosenblatt
The Playhouse Near Dark, Elizabeth Holmes
Drift and Pulse, Kathleen Halme
Black Threads, Jeff Friedman

2008

The Grace of Necessity, Samuel Green
After West, James Harms
The Book of Sleep, Eleanor Stanford
Anticipate the Coming Reservoir, John Hoppenthaler
Parable Hunter, Ricardo Pau-Llosa
Convertible Night, Flurry of Stones, Dzvinia Orlowsky